Enjoy!

:)

# *The* HONEST TRUTH *about* LEADERSHIP

## PEG BUEHRLE
## PETE MCDOWELL

# WHAT OTHERS ARE SAYING ABOUT PEG & PETE AND THEIR STRATEGIES

"Peg & Pete have helped me grow my business, hone my leadership skills, gain confidence, and develop my team into better leaders. They've also aligned my team to reach toward the same goals."

**Amy Brogan,** President, Kelley Dental Laboratory

"Peg and Pete have been an integral part of our leadership development. They are extremely engaged in our business, and we always feel they approach our issues as if they were issues of their own. Not only do they coach our leadership team and emerging leaders throughout the year, but they are also part of our annual two-day retreat, where we set our long and short-term goals. We would not be able to get through what we do in as efficient of a manner without their guidance. Peg and Pete are advisors, coaches, and friends of M+A. We are forever grateful for their commitment to our success!"

**Carrie Boyd,** Managing Principal, M+A Architects

"I think the biggest thing Pete has done for us gives us the power to give ourselves permission to work ON the business instead of IN the business on a daily basis. By doing that, we were able to focus on the management team and give them the tools they need to run the business for us, allowing us the freedom not to be there EVERY day. It's a work in progress, and making an effort to maintain a positive and supportive culture and coaching the management team has been a game-changer for the business and our personal lives."

**Sarah Himelstein,** Co-Owner, Puptown Lounge

"I'd like to take this opportunity to thank Peg and Pete of ActionCOACH for the positive impact their valuable coaching had on my team and me. They helped us identify and focus on what is really important for success in our business and our personal lives. One important leadership lesson learned was it's not your title that makes you a leader; it's how you treat those you lead and help them grow. When you foster mutual trust – they will follow you because they *want* to, not because they *have* to. Today our business is thriving, and our company culture is better than ever. We would not be where we are today without the positive influence of Peg and Pete's coaching."

**Dave Hawkins,** President, Paul J. Ford & Company

Peg and Pete have been in the business of helping business owners for over 16 years. They deal with major issues as you're growing your business, like getting the right Leadership, helping increase sales, and increasing the value of your business. Maybe you're in the succession time in your business, and you need some expert advice there. They are amazing folks, and they can help your business succeed, grow, and be profitable. The value of your business will grow with the right people on your team like Pete and Peg.

**Kevin Harrington,** Entrepreneur, Original Shark on Shark Tank

"The longer you wait to hire a coach, the longer you will have to wait to reach your goals. You can get there, but you will get there a lot quicker when you have the guidance, the knowledge, and the resources that Peg can bring. When you face your challenges, Peg will help you to create a plan to move forward. You will see improvement and gain confidence as you execute your plan. So, do not wait. Bring Peg on, get some coaching, and her team will help you achieve your goals."

**Aaron Enfinger,** Chief Operating Officer, The Cleary Company

"I love working with Peg & Pete. Their entire team has been awesome to work with. We are in the relationship business, and having a relationship with them is fruitful in many ways. We have traveled across the country to ActionCOACH meetings, attended world-class seminars, heard incredible world-renowned speakers, and enjoyed lots of fun times together. In the six years we have been working with Peg, our sales and staff have quadrupled, and my mental state and financial state have remained high and flourished. We have been through some great coaching sessions and achieved many high points in our business in the past 5-6 years. I have referred Peg & Pete a dozen times or more in that timeframe and will continue to do this because of their results. Whether it's Leadership, management training, culture, finances, figuring out how to move your location or expand to another location, these great folks will have your back. We surely wouldn't have had the success we have had without the guidance of Peg & Pete. I am not sure I could have done this without their help."

**George Cleary,** Owner, The Cleary Company

"When I first met Pete, I was initially impressed with Pete's enthusiasm, communication skills, and professional demeanor. Since that initial meeting, Pete has consistently demonstrated all of these qualities and more, and I heartily endorse him to work with your organization. Of particular value to me as a client was Pete's enthusiastic embrace of change, ability to develop creative solutions, and unwavering commitment to exceeding my expectations. I regularly receive unsolicited feedback from my team commending Pete's outstanding level of service, professionalism, and follow-through. Pete has my highest recommendation to work with your company.

**Mark Miller,** President, Lion's Den

"Without their help, I would never have made the best decision I ever made for my business."

**Ryan Puckett,** Partner, Skylight Financial Group

"After ten years of being an employee in my business, Peg and Pete have taught me how to have my business work for me. From the beginning, we laid out our mission and values and dedicated time and effort into establishing our culture, which really is our competitive edge."

**Cliff Boyden,** Co-Owner, Puptown Lounge

"Peg and Pete have been instrumental for our company. They have helped identify opportunities, create a game plan, and implement critical cultural changes needed for the team to flourish. We have since seen team members go from zeroes to heroes to help drive the company's growth instead of the owners pulling the team uphill."

**Andrew Schroeder,** Owner, Schroeder Design Build Remodel

"Peg is a rock star, pure and simple. I have been working with Peg for several years, and our business has grown over 250%. More importantly, we have grown with the grace and presence of also improving our client service! Peg brings a positive attitude in everything she does, from challenging the status quo to helping us reach new heights. I highly recommend Peg and her team!"

**Jef Forward,** Owner, Forward Design Build Remodel

"We were introduced to Peg by a friend and never imagined how much she would help us! She is wise, intelligent, and kind but also so practical. She doesn't just tell us things to do but helps us create systems to make things really happen! Her encouragement and support -- even through the hard times -- have made a true impact on us. She really cares and shows it!"

**Dr. Carey Girgis,** Owner, Back Pain Relief Ohio

"Peg & Pete have helped us to improve our firm for many years. They have shown us how to become more profitable while creating a team culture we are extremely proud of. They have also helped us to hire and retain some of the best talent in the business."

**Brant Poling,** Owner & CEO Poling Law

"I have worked with Peg & Pete since 2008. In that time, we have tripled in size and created a business that can work without me. As a result, I am now able to work on the parts of my business that I enjoy the most!"

**James Green,** Owner & CEO of Ohio Exteriors

"I have worked with Peg & Pete for over ten years. They have helped me as a leader with my ability to focus and maintain a positive outlook that affects my entire team. They have helped us become more effective as a team by obtaining alignment, ensuring open and honest communication. This has led to consistent improvement in business results."

**Rick Schmeltzer,** COO of Air Force One

"I have worked with Peg and Pete steadily since 2008. During this time, our firm and team have tripled in size. We have created a culture of continuous improvement, and we attract great employees to our firm. They have also helped me to create a logical and effective succession plan. I am happy to say the plan is working to provide financial security not only for myself but for the next generation of owners who currently work in my business."

**Julie Daniels,** Owner & CEO of
Ed's Heating, Cooling, Plumbing & Electric

# SHARE THE GIFT OF LEADERSHIP

## BULK ORDERING AVAILABLE

RETAIL PRICE $24.95

| | |
|---|---|
| 5-20 Books | $19.99 each |
| 20-99 Books | $17.99 each |
| 100-499 Books | $14.99 each |
| 500+ Books | $9.99 Each |

To our Families:
Who make the world a better place,
Who inspire us every day to be our best, and
For their unwavering support.

To You, the Reader:
For your commitment to self-improvement.
We're proud of you!

To our Clients, our Team, and Fans:
Your support has made this book possible.

# CONTENTS

# FOREWORD

**Allow Me to Introduce Myself**

My name is Mark Daniels, and for more than two decades, I've proudly held the position of President of M+A Architects. At M+A Architects, we are driven by our vision of enriching lives through innovative design. We work every day to enhance communities, elevate human experiences, and define a sustainable future. A preeminent architectural firm in the Midwest, M+A has a national presence, with offices in Columbus and Cincinnati, Ohio. Founded in 1980, with over 100 employees, the firm serves nine specialty sectors, driven by a studio of industry experts whose passion drives their focus on function, style, and trends relative to their specific market. Our award-winning firm specializes in healthcare, workplace, mixed-use, higher education, community, and multifamily, including senior living and workforce housing.

A range of complementary services to architecture includes strategic and master planning, interior design, an innovative change management program, and an in-house experiential design and production team.

Beyond what we do, I am particularly proud of who we are, with a strong Corporate + Social Responsibility program demonstrating our deeply rooted commitment to the cities and communities we work and live in, as well as a dedicated Sustainability team and program, to create a healthier future for tomorrow, today. We have achieved national recognition by selection as the Best Place to Work, Best Company Culture, and Best Community Involvement.

### History + Happenstance

I was born and raised in Columbus, Ohio. I am a proud alumnus of The Ohio State University and a huge supporter of all things Columbus. Of the amazing things our city has to offer, one of the greatest is my wife, Julie Broerman Daniels, and my children. My proudest accomplishment being the adults they have become.

Julie and I both serve as CEOs of our respective companies (hers being Ed's Heating Cooling Plumbing Electric–a longstanding client of Peg and Pete's). Julie and I connected on a boat ride on the Scioto River with Peg and Pete some years ago.

### Peg, Pete and the Path to Potential

From the day we enlisted Peg and Pete as the official business, executive, and Leadership coaches of M+A, to today, thirteen years later, their partnership has positioned M+A for optimal success on the path to our greatest potential.

In 2008, I anticipated the threat of a looming recession and the inevitable impact on our industry. To be proactive, I decided to brace for impact and introduced Peg and Pete to the firm's operations. What many leadership coaches would have seen as a significant obstacle, they found as an opportunity, not shying away in the face of a challenge but recognizing the potential for change. As the building and design world and the general economy as a whole began to shatter, we remained strategic.

With Peg and Pete's guidance, we navigated the recession with as much resiliency as possible, making difficult decisions with great thought and purpose. It was Peg and Pete we turned to in order to grow the firm from the 38 remaining associates to the over 100 top-tier talent we have working with the firm today.

Pete & Peg's global awards of recognition for "Longest Client Retention" multiple times aren't a coincidence but indicative of the confidence, respect, and trust they earn with every working relationship they have and the proven value they demonstrate.

As a results-driven President, their value is non-negotiable and imperative for the success of our firm.

### The Value of Peg and Pete to Our Vision

Among their value add within the firm, Peg and Pete support the vision and success of M+A through efforts like:

- Executive Coaching for Individuals
- Succession Planning + Training for Future Leaders
- Facilitation of Quarterly Sessions
- Annual Planning Retreat for Principals

Just some of the areas Peg and Pete help us with are:

- Interpersonal skills
- Emotional intelligence
- Time management
- Delegation
- Succession planning

- On-boarding
- Employee retention
- General management

In a competitive industry, their aid in hiring top-tier talent has proven incredibly valuable, helping us curate the strongest team possible with some of the best talent in the industry.

## This Book's Journey For You

This book is laid out in a way that starts with you—the same way Peg and Pete approach their coaching, intentionally. Creating a positive, encouraging, forgiving and learning-driven environment for yourself allows you to become the best leader you can be. A great leader knows you have to put your oxygen mask on first because developing a great team and a great company begins with a great leader.

Your next great team members will be attracted to your organization by doing the work that is laid out in this simple yet elegant text. Each chapter will present a principle, explain why it applies, then give you a small piece of homework. You may read through the book once and then begin the homework.

My suggestion is to read one chapter at a time—taking time to reflect on what you have learned, and then complete the "homework." Take 1-2 weeks to do this for each chapter to allow the lessons and learnings to resonate. As with all long-lasting change, small incremental work will produce the best and most permanent results.

Peg and Pete are great at what they do because of who they are. Let them guide you to use "The Honest Truth" principles to become the Leader you know you can be.

### In Closing

During the most challenging time of my life–both personally and professionally–Peg and Pete came into my world, and suddenly things began to shift. Opportunities I hadn't seen before became apparent, challenges turned into opportunities, and I found my newly lifted spirits serve me individually and the firm collectively.

While Peg and Pete began as my coaches, I am proud to say they have become my lifelong friends. I am grateful for their guidance and proud of our unlocked potential and possibilities through our partnership.

If the past is any indication of the future, the best is yet to come through our partnership, and the same will be true for you.

*Mark Daniels*
President
M+A Architects

# THE TRUTH
# TRIANGLE

AS BUSINESS OWNERS, we tend to want to start with the business. Of course – this is something to which you have given your life, your financial security, and your legacy. But to make the business function at the highest level and get to the top of the mountain, the base of everything you do is rooted in your skills, mindset, habits, and beliefs as a leader. If those leadership skills – learned skills, not inherited talents – are not strong enough to support your efforts, the business can come crumbling down. This Honest Truth is why we begin this book focusing on you as a leader, not on the business or even your team.

Your skills as a leader will show up in the team that you attract, and ultimately the long-term results of your team. The second section is "US" because an iron-clad team culture is the greatest asset in your business's success. It's been proven repeatedly that happy teams produce the best results, and this fact is shown in the companies of our clients every day. The teams we coach have won global, national, and local awards for Team Culture and Best Places to Work over and over again for a reason: they have committed to not only personal success but the success of the team.

Once the foundation is strong and you've climbed the truth triangle, navigating plateaus and setbacks along the way, then it's time to put the pedal to the metal on growing your business. Your development is the force multiplier that will improve results with less and less effort over time.

# PART 1
# YOU

# CHAPTER 1
# LEADERSHIP STYLE

HAVE YOU EVER taken a step back and looked at your leadership style? Have you ever considered how you could best help your peers, your team, and your company as a leader?

After a coaching session with a small business owner, this business owner instantly realized why their business was suffering and continued to have problems. That cause? The Owner's Leadership. The coaching session lasted only half of the allotted time—the Business Owner ended the session by saying, "I know what I have to do. It's me. I own it." As a result of that ownership of the leadership style, their business has nearly tripled in the few years that they have been a client, and the Owner is happy, healthy, and their team is thriving.

Deciding which leadership behaviors you intentionally concentrate on will help your relationships with your teammates and peers and bring the whole organization up a level.

There are five types of leaders who own the businesses that we coach. Consider this list and think about where you are currently.

1. **The Beginning Leader.** The Beginning Leader is generally working too much, making too little, stressed, and overwhelmed. Their businesses are often not profitable, and if they are, the Leader

is working double-time to make it happen. The Beginning Leader generally has high employee turnover. They are consistently losing team members to better opportunities and hiring again. Except for a select few team members, the team that works for the Beginning Leader has worked for them less than a year and is constantly looking for a better opportunity. Being a Beginning Leader for a long time will be exhausting and may affect your health and personal relationships. Often Beginning Leaders don't empower their team enough and don't see a clear better way. The common phrase uttered by a Beginning Leader is "I know," or they know best and are not willing to grow.

2. **The Emerging Leader.** The Emerging Leader is generally a leader with a few great strengths that have taken them far but have not nearly reached their potential. There are a few things that are holding them back. Typically, the Emerging Leader works too much *in* the business and needs to move beyond that to work *on* the business. Emerging Leaders have teams that depend on them to make all decisions; they take on too much and work more than full time to complete the tasks at hand. Emerging Leaders are on their way to burnout in their roles, often have stress-related illnesses, and have unhappy teams. Negativity on most of the team has crept in, but it's not too late to turn those existing teams around.

3.  **The Average Leader.** The Average Leader
    has learned some essential lessons already and
    understands the value of lifelong learning. They
    have generally established some successful systems,
    they have a seasoned, established team, and the
    business is stable. The team comes to work and gets
    the job done every day, but turnover happens more
    than you would like. The leaders in the business are
    working hard, and they have taken some strides to
    plan for the company's success. This is the point at
    which leaders can see the potential for exponential
    business growth. The business owner may know
    that the business can indeed be profitable, but
    they have reached a plateau. Growth of 1-5% is
    happening, but life would look much brighter if
    you could get to 10-20% growth year over year
    without sacrificing quality and maintaining or
    growing profit margins.

4.  **The Successful Leader.** The Successful Leader
    has a strong, happy team. They're working less
    than they ever thought possible. They likely went
    on a vacation, even multiple vacations, this year
    because they could step away from the business,
    and it made money without them. Successful
    Leaders have taken time to work *on* their business,
    not constantly *in* their business, and the company is
    successful because of it. The team culture is positive,
    and the customers are reaping the benefits. Here's

where your leadership development pays off. You've developed yourself as a leader, so it's time to create the future leaders for your team. You have an end game in mind, and you're ready to have a viable business to sell or transfer to your successor without worry. Even though they've made it to the top of the curve, successful leaders have a never-ending quest for learning and are continuously improving.

5.  **The Expert Leader.** The Expert Leader has made it. They are filling only the roles in their business that they genuinely enjoy, their business is growing double digits year over year, and their team has called this place their home until retirement. Each team member understands exactly what they need to do to get the job done, and they happily do that and more. Every system is in place, and every process is documented. The business owner can sit back, relax, and enjoy the fruits of their labor. Something truly marvelous happens to the Expert Leader, however. Even though they have made it to the very top of their game, they have an insatiable desire to be more and do more. Learning and growing have become such a part of their lives that shutting it off becomes impossible. Expert Leaders are now learning and growing so their teams can learn and grow. They naturally attract and retain like-minded individuals.

Want to find out where you are on our Leadership Behaviors scale? Take the test for free on our website today:

http://honesttruthbook.com or scan the QR Code below:

# LET'S TAKE ACTION

- Look at the skills, the knowledge and the attitude that it requires in order to be a great leader. Think of leaders that you admire as examples.

- Write these characteristics down on a list and rank your own abilities with each one.

- Select one with a low ranking and decide what is it that you need to do to improve. Some examples of these characteristics could be having a positive attitude, being a great communicator, being inspirational, or being a good listener.

- Take the Leadership Behaviors Test in the link provided. This will give you a starting position!

# CHAPTER 2
# YOUR STYLE AND DISC BEHAVIORS

RECENTLY, WE WERE coaching an executive on improving rapport with employees, both ones that did and didn't report to her. We had seen a gap in connection between her and the team. One of our first questions was, "have you thought about adapting your approach to each person's behavior profile?" It's essential to understand how each person is wired and tailor interactions based on that behavior type. Adapting your communication will make each interaction more meaningful and lead to solid relationships.

There are many personality-type tests in the market today, but we often use DiSC. The DiSC Behavior Profile is a personality behavior system based on theories dating back as far as 444 BC when the pre-Socratic Greek philosopher Empedocles documented that people acted in 4 distinctly different ways. He tied these personalities to Earth, Wind, Fire, and Water. Fast forward to 1928, William Moulton Martin theorized in his book *Emotions of Normal People* that there are four personality quadrants described as Dominance, Influence, Steadiness, and Compliance (DISC).

- Dominance personalities are often described as "driven," moving fast and driven by results.

- Influencers are fast-moving with an emphasis on people & fun.

- Steadiness is characterized by sensitivity and introversion.

- Compliance personalities are very detail-oriented and inspired by process.

It's important to remember that you can be a highly successful leader regardless of your personality type. Most people have traits of a couple, or even all, styles. Each of these traits is extremely valuable.

As a leader, making sure you meet your team where they are and adjusting your leadership style to what *they* need is essential for effective Leadership. The strength of your connection will improve when you take the time to practice this technique.

# LET'S TAKE ACTION

- Complete a DISC profile analysis for yourself. (these assessments are available through our website, www.honesttruthbook.com)

- Share the results with a key co-worker or significant other.

- Have your key employees take the assessment and hold a meeting to share the results. Better yet, hire a third-party DISC expert to facilitate this meeting. Our experienced team can facilitate these virtually.

- CHALLENGE: Identify the profile you are least like and practice being that person for 5-10 minutes. This exercise will be uncomfortable at first but will get you on the path to adjusting automatically when working anyone.

- Recommended reference—People Smart in Business, 2006, by Tony Alessandra, PhD., Michael J. O'Connor, PhD., and Janice Van Dyke, PhD.

# CHAPTER 3
# SELF-CARE

STAYING POSITIVE AS a leader is essential in performing your job. To make sure you stay positive, we have five pillars of self-care that we as coaches practice with our teams, managers, and leaders.

The Five Pillars are:

1. Consistent Learning. Make sure that you're continually growing. Our brains are built to get rid of synapses that are not needed, as an energy-saving measure, causing our cognitive functions to slip after we graduate from college or cut back our workload near retirement. A consistent habit of learning is proven to increase life expectancy and certainly cognitive ability in that life.

2. Meditation. Regular meditation reduces stress and negative thoughts. It needs to be a part of your life. Get a meditation app or meditation audio of some kind to be able to shut your brain down just for a few minutes to recoup and recharge.

3. Exercise. Whether you walk, run, bike, swim, lift, or dance, exercise has a positive effect on not only your body but your brain. What exercise is best? The one that you will *do*. The endorphins released when you exercise have been proven to increase positive outlook and decrease depression.

4. Affirmations. What you say to yourself about yourself when you're by yourself can affect your outlook on every facet of your life. Saying out loud what you believe to be true about your present or future can reprogram your brain for positive thinking. Try things like "I am a successful leader." or "I have great ideas that people want to hear." It may feel uncomfortable at first to say these statements aloud, but keep going. If you're not quite where you want to be, use "in the process." For example, if you're not at your goal weight, say, "I am in the process of losing weight so I can enjoy life and have more confidence."

5. Gratitude. Start your day being grateful for what you have and where you are. One of the easiest ways to do this is a gratitude snooze. Instead of falling back asleep after your alarm goes off, take that time to think of the things going well in your life. Try writing in a gratitude journal, capturing why you are grateful for the people, circumstances, and experiences around you. Multiple scientific studies have concluded that cultivating the habit of gratitude influences not only your mental health but your sleep health, physical health, and health of your relationships.

Creating a culture of positivity starts with the leaders. In all of these positive habits, show your team the way and lead by example.

# LET'S TAKE ACTION

- Pick one of the self-care strategies and implement. Your goal is to do all 5 consistently!

# CHAPTER 4
# PATIENCE = LOVE

ONE OF MY happiest memories, when the kids were younger, was teaching each of them to ride a bike. Many of you have done this. What a thrill! You stand beside them as they are excitedly sitting on the bike. You put one hand on a handlebar, one hand on the back of the seat, and slowly start to move. As you get started, you talk to them in positive, encouraging words, in a kind tone of voice. At some point, as they are pedaling along, you let go and let them go on their own. Sometimes they fall. You patiently help them to gather their courage to try again.

Just like we did with our kids, we want to have great patience with our employees. They are going to have challenges at home and work. When you consistently demonstrate patience with your employees and focus on PROGRESS, not PERFECTION, they will know that you care about them. When you love them as a person by showing patience, you will get their best every day!

# LET'S TAKE ACTION

- At the end of your week, think back and ask yourself "when did I show great patience with someone?" Remember that feeling.

# CHAPTER 5
# FEAR

WE ALL GET into situations where we are afraid to take action from time to time. Yet, decisive action can make or break the health of your business. Fear is a common reason to decide against taking action. However, facing your fears is sometimes the only way to make a crucial decision.

One example we often see is a leader with an employee who has annoying behavior right now but left unchecked could be destructive to your customer's experience. If you let fear take over and fail to address a small drip, then you could have a flood on your hands very quickly.

Another common problem we see is what we call Scope Creep. Everyone has a client that takes more and more of your time and demands more and more of your services but is still paying the same amount. You have a responsibility to the business to address the additional services, raise their pricing structure, or end the relationship. There are many ways to manage this and keep your customer happy. Often, the client has no idea that they are receiving services for which they are not paying.

# LET'S TAKE ACTION

- Make a list of the conversations you have delayed having. Also make a list of the prices that need to be raised.

- Next to each, put a date. Mark them in the calendar.

- Have a trusted friend, coach, or coworker hold you accountable to having that conversation on that date. Facing your fear through accountability gets easier every time!

# CHAPTER 6
# HANDLING NEGATIVITY

AS LEADERS, WE are called on to help employees, clients, or sub-contractors overcome negativity when they get into an uncomfortable situation. If you have a generally positive employee who suddenly comes in negative, they may need your help to talk it through. Just by asking "what's wrong?" or "what can we do right now that would be most helpful to make your day better" shows that you care and may be what they need to hear. Listening, without judgment, could be the best approach. You may be able to help them leave problems from home at home when they come to work. You may also help them gain the confidence they need to take positive action toward solving a problem. Taking the time to listen empathetically may be all they need to move forward.

Remember, *you get what you tolerate*. When you address negativity with compassion, you will go a long way toward helping someone move forward. For the consistently negative employee, the path forward is quite different. It is up to you to determine if this person is willing to learn that there is a better way, ready to change, and will follow through on creating a more positive mindset for themselves. If the answer is a firm no to any of these three questions, it may be time for this person to move on.

# LET'S
# TAKE ACTION

- Positivity is one of the most needed assets for leading. Rate your own positivity index on a scale of 1-10 and determine what you need to do to increase it.

- A Positivity Index tool is available on our website, http://honesttruthbook.com/resources

- Looking at our chapter on self-care, which pillars are you doing and how often? Use these strategies to increase your positivity index.

# CHAPTER 7
# HAPPINESS COMES FROM ACCEPTANCE

ONE OF THE great things that leaders can do for themselves is accept things as they are. It does not mean giving up or lowering your standards. It does mean that the people in your organization including your employees, clients, and sub-contractors have a specific background, skillset, behavior profile, and view of the world that defines where they are today. After you accept the person for who they are, you can get to work to help them be their best.

The other acceptance, with no less importance, is the acceptance of yourself and the current state of your business today. You have arrived here through all of the previous decisions you have made or not made over the years. Acceptance of today provides a strong foundation from which you can propel yourself and the business forward. Give yourself and your companions a break, and set your path for today, this week, and this month. This is the path to happiness.

# LET'S
# TAKE ACTION

- Write down the things with which you are struggling.

- Decide if this is a style difference or will it affect the outcome.

- Make a conscious decision to let go of the things that will not affect the outcome.

# CHAPTER 8

# GROWTH COMES FROM CHANGE

CHANGE IS, AT times, a four-letter word. It's scary! As a leader, you must realize that personal and professional growth comes from changing how you do things. This can start with your perspective when things go wrong. Is this a problem or an opportunity for us to improve? Evaluate your mindset the next time an employee does not complete a project in the way you expected. If your first instinct is to blame, make excuses, or deny, a change of perspective could make all the difference. Instead of "that person is wreaking havoc on our company" or "they're a bad employee," think, "I hired this person for a reason." As a leader, take ownership of the situation.

After all, in many cases, you selected this employee, onboarded them, trained them, and provided positive reinforcement while they learned about their role and your organization. This type of ownership of the success of each employee will give you and your team an edge in a competitive world.

# LET'S TAKE ACTION

- As you go through your day today, look for ways to view things from an "opportunity" perspective.

- Beginning with yourself, change the way you react to it!

# CHAPTER 9
# BABY STEPS

WHILE COACHING OUR executives and businesses, we have taught each client a similar way of thinking. Have you ever been told that you need to change? What is your initial reaction? If you are like us, the prospect of changing yourself is intimidating. Where do I start? How am I possibly going to change?

By avoiding the word "change" in coaching and mentoring, we can remove a common mental barrier that personal improvement is difficult.

Is change difficult at times? Sure.

Is change uncomfortable at times? Definitely.

Creating a habit of embracing change is one of the most potent examples a leader can set.

Focusing on small, incremental steps over shorter periods is more achievable than a life-altering dramatic change. It allows you to set consistent habits for the long term without taking a massive leap in the beginning.

For example, if we start exercising, we would not start by running a marathon! The first step could be walking 30 minutes twice a week. Once this becomes an ingrained habit (you would not feel right if you missed it), you are ready to up the ante. The real secret is to "just" get 1% better every day. If you exercised just 15 minutes and increased it by 1% every day, at the end of 100 days, you would be up to 40 minutes! In the meantime, you get to win every day – that first day's improvement is a mere 9 seconds.

Improvement comes from establishing habits that repeat over time. Achieving lasting and dramatic growth comes from that type of change.

# LET'S
# TAKE ACTION

- Select one business habit on which you will improve.

- Using our example, identify the first incremental (achievable) steps you will take each day to improve.

- After 21 days, when the change has become natural, reward yourself! Decide if this habit deserves more incremental change or select a new one and repeat the process.

# CHAPTER 10

# TUNE OUT THE SMALL STUFF

GREAT LEADERS WILL sometimes "tune out" small things to keep their eye on the prize. Letting go of some small things that are not exactly up to snuff allows you to focus on the most important goals. Let your employees make a mistake now and then. Now, if they are driving the company bus over a cliff, you may want to tap the brakes a bit.

In many cases, you can back up and observe what is going on and not get involved. When you let small things go, you may get more buy-in when you do intercede. Whatever gets your attention, energy and focus grows. Make sure your attention is on the critical things, the things in your company that only you can do. Say "no" to the small stuff or even better, empower an employee to own that task.

# LET'S
# TAKE ACTION

- Take a week and make a list of the situations with which you got involved.

- Ask yourself the question, did I need to get involved with that situation?

- When you do this over time, you will find yourself focused on higher value interactions.

# CHAPTER 11
# INDECISION IS NO DECISION

QUICK, SMART DECISIONS are a hallmark of a great leader and is a success-making habit. Remember, plans can always be adjusted and adapted to what is happening after making the decision.

When we see businesses and leaders struggle, they have put off choices that they know they need to be making. It is this indecision that can get you in the end.

We have one company that put off a personnel decision to terminate an employee for a year. It nearly put them out of business. The business was a complete turnaround and is very successful due to executing that decision that they knew needed to happen. *You* may be the one holding you back. *You* may be the one holding your company back.

# LET'S TAKE ACTION

- Make a list of the decisions you know you should be making or that you've delayed making. (firing a toxic employee, expanding a physical facility, or creating a new position.

- Just like the tough conversations, put a deadline in the calendar when the decision needs to be made. Commit to the timing, make the decision, and move on.

# CHAPTER 12
# IT'S OK NOT TO BE LIKED

THE HONEST TRUTH: as a leader you will not always make people happy. Your job is to protect your department, employees, and company. Not everybody is going to agree with you, and that is okay.

We often ask our Executive Coaching clients, "how often are people agreeing with you" and "how often are you upsetting people"? While it's not a sign of a great leader to have everyone always upset and dislike you, giving feedback and holding teams accountable is an essential part of every Leader's job. What is most vital for you to understand is that you are the protector of the business, and as the Leader, you have been charged with making the tough decisions. Sometimes that's not always the popular decision.

Keep your focus on the organization's mission, vision, and goals. Keep your team in the loop on those goals. Remember, as a leader, not everybody will like you, and you must embrace that.

# LET'S TAKE ACTION

- Self-reflection: For the next three weeks, at the end of each week, ask yourself was the feedback primarily negative or positive about the decisions that I made.

# PART 2
# US

# CHAPTER 13
# WHY

A LEADER MUST understand why each employee comes to work every day. It is not just because they need money! They do something in their off time that drives them to succeed at work. It could be family, pets, travel, vacations, children, hobbies, home repairs, learning, music, or in most cases, a uniquely personal combination. Great leaders understand each employee's "reason for being."

When you gain this understanding, you will have insight into creating buy-in with each team member. When you figure this out, you will develop a team of powerfully motivated people to ensure that their needs coincide with your needs. You will get more done with less effort cheerfully and positively.

# LET'S
# TAKE ACTION

- List the "critical" employees (the list could include clients or trade partners) in your work world (5-7 is a good number).

- Determine if you truly know them well enough to understand their "why"

- Take action to get to know those individuals that you scored the lowest on your list.

# CHAPTER 14
# LEADING UP

WE HAVE ALL been in a situation where we have had a superior in our organization do something that is not good for the group. This could be the CEO, Board Chairperson, President, or even a significant client. Will this situation, if left alone, negatively affect the business? If the answer is yes, it must be addressed. Whether or not you believe it, you are in a position to offer counsel and, potentially, solutions to anyone, even the boss.

How? First, privately, professionally, and with a clear business purpose in mind, address the situation. State what you have personally observed and why you believe it is essential to address. It can't be a case of "Sam told me that Terry is saying inappropriate things to another employee." It must be "I observed Terry saying XYZ to another employee." Use a specific first-hand example that takes the emotion out of it.

Take the role of a coach. If possible, help them identify the various options available, select a path, and make a commitment to act. If asked, you can provide your suggestions. The more significant their role in choosing the solution, the more committed they will be to taking positive action. You may also want to ask them if they would like you to provide them feedback in the future. Feedback from a trusted and respected subordinate is invaluable to any leader.

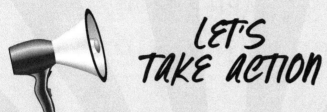

# LET'S TAKE ACTION

- Identify any "lead up" conversations you need to have and the desired outcome.

- Pick one conversation on which you will take action.

# CHAPTER 15
# SITUATIONAL LEADERSHIP

THE MOST EFFECTIVE leaders have many qualities in common, but we consistently see the ability to adjust effortlessly. Not every employee or boss needs the same direction or emotional support level. Different tasks may require more or less support even with the same employee.

Researchers Paul Hershey and Ken Blanchard coined the term Situational Leadership in their 1969 book *Management of Organizational Behavior*. The fundamental principle of the situational leadership model is that there is no single "best" style of Leadership. It is choosing the right leadership style for the right task with each person.

When assigning a task or delegating to an employee, think about the job and the person's skill level with respect to the task. Also, consider the level of confidence they have relative to this task. Once a person is highly motivated and highly capable, you will be able to delegate freely. You will know that the job will be done efficiently, effectively, and on time. Until this happens, it is up to you to manage the amount of directive behavior and emotional support this employee needs. When you do this well, you will complete the task and develop the skill and self-confidence of your employee!

# LET'S TAKE ACTION

- Read the article Situational Leadership. A link to the article is on our website, www.honesttruthbook.com/resources

- What are the next three things you are going to delegate?

- Determine what your leadership style should be in each of these cases.

- Once they have completed the tasks, do a self-evaluation on how it worked.

# CHAPTER 16
# IS ANYBODY LISTENING?

AS WE TALK to managers and business owners, we get that question often. Here's the honest truth: your team is not listening because you've been saying the same thing again and again, in the same way. It's like they've just tuned you out. You have not tailored your message to the audience.

We suggest bringing in an outside voice to communicate the message because the message is naturally presented differently. We've acted as the facilitator, communicator, and intermediary hundreds of times with many different businesses as coaches. Sometimes when we interrupt what has been happening over a long period and get to the root of the problem, the team can see it for the first time.

This frustrating process can also be liberating. Your team can finally listen to the things they need to do and take the actions they need to take for you to see success! Once the hard work of bringing in an outsider is done and the message is clearly heard, you and the team can move forward and complete your mission.

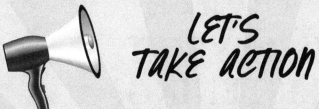

# LET'S TAKE ACTION

- Consider the method you are using to communicate. If an e-mail didn't work try a phone call, if a phone call doesn't work try face to face.

- Consider having someone else deliver the message

# CHAPTER 17
# CONFLICT

NO ONE ACTUALLY enjoys conflict. When it comes to the success of the business or team, avoiding conflict could be detrimental. We suggest that our leaders actually seek out conflict when the topic is important enough for the organization. If you have two departments with a disagreement about how things are handled, it is inevitable that at some point, you may need to sit down with both groups.

As a leader, you can facilitate a calm discussion that gets the facts out on the table for all to examine. You can help find points of agreement, clarify differences in terms of the organization's success, and keep the discussion positive.

Abraham Lincoln was very skilled in allowing conflict within his cabinet. After being elected president, he appointed some of his fiercest political rivals as his cabinet members. As a leader, we encourage you to engage in conflict when needed, keeping the organization's key objectives in mind as you help reach an agreement.

# LET'S TAKE ACTION

- Write down the unresolved conflicts that you know are occurring in your business.

- Prioritize them

- Engage in a solution one by one.

# CHAPTER 18
# TRUST

AS LEADERS, WE all want people to trust us. The best way to get this done is to be trustworthy: be the one that your team can count on to do what you say you will do. Take a look in the mirror and make sure that you act so that people will naturally trust you.

According to psychologist Patrick Sweeney, the three pillars of building trust are the 3 C's: Character, Competence, and Connection (he used the term "Caring"). Your Character is on display every day as you make consistent decisions for the right reasons every day. Your Competence is shown as you use your skills and ability to guide the team in managing business challenges. Knowing the limits of your skills and acknowledging that is crucial too. Lastly, you must also make a personal Connection to each individual in your group to fully gain their trust. When this connection is strong, your team members will give their best without hesitation.

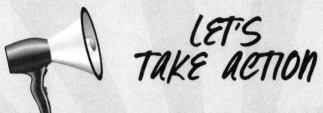

# LET'S TAKE ACTION

- Make a list of your key relationships.

- Rank each relationship, in terms of the 3 C's, 1-10.

- Start improving one relationship a time.

# CHAPTER 19
# CLEAR EXPECTATIONS

ONE OF THE fun things about being a leader is setting expectations for new employees or existing employees doing new things. Meeting with an individual to discuss the desired project outcome and the different ways to approach the assignment is an excellent investment of your time. Depending on the specific experience level of the employee, you may adjust how you help them decide what steps to take first. Regardless, a discussion of all aspects of the completed project is essential. You may also need to discuss boundaries (time & money), involvement with other departments, milestones, and points when you expect communication.

Aside from task management, another crucial area for setting expectations is in the area of behavior. If one of your values is teamwork, have a detailed discussion about what that means in practice. For example, you may say a great team member

- Helps when someone is struggling
- Completes work at or on deadlines
- Communicates early when they cannot meet a deadline

- Remembers that it is better to be kind than to be right

- Stays positive as much as possible

By being clear about your expectations, holding employees accountable to those expectations becomes much more manageable.

# LET'S
# TAKE ACTION

- Write down the behavior expectations you have for all of your team members.

- Make a list of every team member and on a scale of 1-10 how each person is doing at achieving those expectations.

- Create a plan on how you can improve the score of each person over time.

# CHAPTER 20
# ALIGNMENT

AS WE WERE coaching one of our executives the other day, she complained about her boss and how they treated her. The boss is the owner, and she is one of the managers of a department. She said that he (the boss) was moving too quickly and was not listening to the team. As a leader in her department, she must seek alignment with her boss and the rest of her team.

Alignment simply means being on the same page with a team, assuring that the team is all headed in the same direction. An alignment allows us to move forward as one because we took a moment to understand each other and what is most important to each person. Lack of alignment leads to wasted energy and sometimes hard feelings.

Executing the alignment process involves allowing each team member to come to the table with their priorities and freely express what is important to them. We recommend using a third-party facilitator, such as a coach, consultant, or mental health professional, to accomplish this. That way, that neutral voice can compile all of the data collected, present a complete vision, and determine guidelines to present the team's vision. The alignment could be between two individuals or for an entire team. For two individuals, the process could be very quick, 15 or 20 minutes, and for a larger group, it could be a day-long event.

Time and time again, aligned teams are shown to be more profitable, have higher revenues, and have happier teams. Employee retention rates increase, and so does production.

# LET'S TAKE ACTION

Look for warning signs from your team (which could include):

- Questions like "Why are we doing that?"

- Fighting

- Unhappy people

- Inconsistent results

# CHAPTER 21
# TRAINING

ARE YOU GUILTY of promoting a manager or Leader and then saying, "here are the keys, now go be a manager"? It is often the case when we walk into organizations that there hasn't been a training or development plan for this newly appointed Leader. Or that we promoted a lot of great employees to supervisors or project managers and never told them how to truly manage people.

One of the essential strategies in developing your organization is to make sure that everyone has a development plan. We want to give them the training and the tools to ensure success. Training your team should be non-negotiable: otherwise, how can you hold them accountable for doing the job well? Establish the standards for the position, provide systems and processes for accomplishing the standards, and, most importantly, regularly check in with the leaders to ensure they understand. Training and development plans are fluid documents – they may change as the business changes. The leaders who prioritize this see the most significant and most consistent growth.

When we see a thorough development and training program, we see a successful company.

# LET'S TAKE ACTION

- Create a spreadsheet, by position, of the skills that are necessary for success.

- Evaluate everyone, on a scale of 1-10, of each person for each skill (you could have other team members and the employee complete this as well.)

- From this, complete an annual development plan for each person.

# CHAPTER 22
# TOUGH CONVERSATIONS

TOUGH CONVERSATIONS ARE essential in ensuring that your team and your team members stay healthy. These conversations are the most challenging part of being a great leader, and we often see even the best leaders delaying these conversations way too long. Holding teams accountable is essential for a successful business.

Make sure when you have those tough conversations that you do it positively. After a positive discussion, you will walk away feeling good about your talk, and they feel like they understand the direction in which they need to go. We always like to say that positive feedback should be like a sandwich:

- The Bun (the soft part): "This is what you've done well."

- The Meat (constructive feedback): "This is what needs to improve."

- The Bun (the soft part): "I believe in you, and I know that you can do this."

# LET'S TAKE ACTION

- Make a list of the specific tough conversations you need to have.

- Prioritize them by how essential they are to the function of the business and write down a date in the calendar that you are going to accomplish the goal.

- Delaying that tough conversation often makes a bad situation worse. Remember, only you can protect your team from poor performance and negativity.

# CHAPTER 23
# ASSUMPTIONS AND EXPECTATIONS

AFTER COACHING TEAMS big and small over the years, one of the most dangerous paths on which we see teams involves two words: *assumptions* and *expectations*. One of the rules we instill with teams as we walk in that first day is to make sure everybody embraces the phrase "*assume positive intent.*"

The brain is wired with a certain "negativity bias." Human brains are built to have a higher sensitivity to negative feelings. Why do you think news programs are filled with doom and gloom? Those stories get the highest ratings. We naturally assume that someone does something because they're out to get us. While this evolved to keep humans safe from danger, it makes for toxic team culture.

You will see a difference if you introduce the phrase "assume positive intent" into your company and consistently hold people accountable to that new thinking. Getting rid of the negative assumptions and the uncommunicated expectations of what you think other people should do will allow your team to be on the same page moving forward. Changing the habits of your team to move toward positive intent will almost always result in change. A positive team and positive results start with positive thinking.

# LET'S TAKE ACTION

- For the next week, actively look for negativity bias and document when you find it.

- After you see the results, decide if you need to emphasize "positive intent" with your team. Remember it starts with you.

# CHAPTER 24
# FEEDBACK

FEEDBACK IS ESSENTIAL to ensure that we are continually growing as a leader. We suggest many different forms of feedback, as some will provide different information than others.

A great place to start is a survey that we call a 360°. It gets its name from the process of asking for feedback from everyone around you. A 360° would be the opportunity for your company or your department to be able to grade you on how you're doing. We recommend that this survey be conducted by a third party – a business coach, consultant, even a psychologist – as employees would be more likely to give an honest answer, and the facilitator can present the results anonymously without resentment.

After the 360° is complete, be honest with your entire team. Be honest about the survey results and the feedback that was given. Be honest about the actions you will take based on what you heard. Acknowledge that although you've had challenges in the past, you are taking specific steps to improve. Don't just let your team feel like they've been heard, allow them to feel like you've listened.

This process works very well in companies and is essential to see growth. In our Executive Coaching program, we work with our executives to help them take significant steps forward, and this is the first one. Big results and big changes have come from this simple process. It's not just the opportunity to ask for feedback, but it's also the opportunity for your team to have a voice in what they see is happening in their culture and with their leaders. Remember, there are two actions that you must address:

1. You're going to change.

2. They see you doing what you say you will do (DWYSYWD).

Working both sides of that equation is essential to see lasting results. Remember Ralph Waldo Emerson's words, "Your actions speak so loudly, I cannot hear what you are saying." Check in with your team often to let them know the results. Remember that perception is reality – if you don't check in with your team, they won't notice. Get credit for all of the hard work and change their perception. This is as important as changing the behavior!

# LET'S TAKE ACTION

- **Make a list of team members whose feedback you would value.**

- Ask these three open ended questions:

- What is the person great at that we want them to continue to do?

- What are this individuals' opportunities for improvement?

- Is there anything else we should know?

- Once the survey is completed, group the similar responses together.

- Evaluate the results and determine what you want to work on.

- Make sure to communicate your plan to those around you.

# CHAPTER 25
# TWO REASONS WHY

ONE OBJECTIVE OF Leadership is helping people to do the things they don't want to do to get to the place they want to be. That's how we coach our clients and how we get long-term results through people. Do you ever wonder why people don't do what you ask? It is *always* one of these two reasons:

- they don't know how
- they don't see the value

Whenever you see your team straying off course, ask yourself whether you've addressed both of these items. Often, when people don't do things correctly, leaders immediately re-train them. If the employees don't see the value, that training will not get your desired results. Make sure your employees understand the importance of what they're doing. As a leader, you must continually assess the adequacy of your training and onboarding processes.

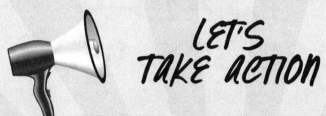

# LET'S TAKE ACTION

- Pick a high value process or step that is not adequately being followed by some of your team.

- Determine which of the reasons above is the root cause (sometimes it is both!)

- Take action to correct.

- Move on to the next opportunity.

# CHAPTER 26
# GETTING BUY-IN

THE OTHER DAY I was talking with an executive that I coach, saying, "if you were in a meeting and somebody came in and said 'this is what you have to do.' How likely are you to get on board?" She said, "not very likely." Exactly. The Leader in that meeting failed to get the group's buy-in. This team doesn't believe in the mission you're promoting and therefore doesn't want to take your suggestions to get there.

As a leader, your job is to get buy-in for ideas and strategies from your team, so they are excited to execute. So how do you get buy-in? You want to make sure that you're making them part of the process and part of the solution. You hired your team for a reason – use the group's ideas to help build the execution of the mission. While we do this, we want the team to understand that we listened and evaluated even if we didn't use the team's idea.

Remember, leaders are salespeople too. You're just "selling" any systems, processes, and changes in the company to the employees. The result of this sales process – showing the team the features and benefits of the new approach – is a team ready to embrace the changes.

Communication is essential in the buy-in process. Once everybody has decided to move forward - we all go arm in arm and charge up that hill together.

# LET'S TAKE ACTION

- As you are thinking about the change, think about who is going to be impacted.

- Ask yourself, have they had an opportunity to weigh in on the change?

- *If an idea is good but can't be used now, make sure you have a parking lot (place to hold ideas for the future) that is visible for all to see.

# CHAPTER 27
# CONSISTENCY

ONE OF THE things that your employees and customers are looking for is consistency from you and your business. People are comforted by the familiar. If your employees have to wonder every day which boss is going to show up – the tyrant or the fun-loving Leader – they will not be secure in their roles. Great leaders have an internal guidance system that helps them to stay consistent. This allows others to remain calm and confident in the direction of the business and you. Treating individuals similarly on a daily basis builds confidence and strengthens relationships over time. Remember to consider the task at hand, the person's developmental level for that task, and the DISC behavior profile of the person you are dealing with each time. This does mean that you may spend more time with one person than another because of differences in individual needs or the task at hand. Remember to hold folks accountable in a consistent manner throughout the organization.

When your team's cultural values and organization's goals are clear, it is a powerful way to allow your employees to make consistent decisions without your input. For example, if customer satisfaction is a high priority in everything you do personally, it will be visible to your employees. When they are faced with a quality or delivery issue, your example will be their guide. Life is a mirror, and your team will reflect your example. Let those reflections be positive ones!

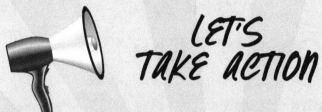

## LET'S TAKE ACTION

- Take a look at your employees and ask yourself a couple of questions – Do I give each person the care, direction and feedback that they need?

- Am I holding everyone accountable to the same standards?

- Once that evaluation is complete, decide the strategies you will take to make sure you are consistent with your team members.

# PART 3
# THE
# BUSINESS

# CHAPTER 28
# VISION

WE ENCOURAGE OUR leaders to have a clear vision of where they are headed. It doesn't matter your level in the organization; having a clear picture of the future will make your journey more accessible and productive. We suggest you start three to five years out and write down a description of what the business will look like at that time. Once done, this will allow you to create a reasonable goal for the company to achieve in one year. We recommend having your plans for the short term in 90-day increments. Ninety days is a long enough time to see measurable results but short enough to focus on the task at hand. A concise 90-Day Plan based on your annual goals will focus your efforts. When you consistently create, work toward and achieve goals through a 90-Day Plan habit, you will be ahead of 90% of the small to mid-sized businesses in the country. Involving your team in developing these visions will create buy-in (less effort from you!) and provide a framework within which they can make great day-to-day decisions. Communicate these plans with the entire team as soon as they are finalized.

# LET'S TAKE ACTION

- Is your vision clear to you and your executive team? If yes—CONGRATULATIONS! If your answer is no, then you have to clarify your vision.

- Walk up to a few team members and ask if they know the vision and/or goals of the company.

- If the three aren't consistent with their answers, then you know you have some work to do!

# CHAPTER 29
# FOCUS

THIS IS ONE of the most important things for your personal and business development. Your brain is wired with a feature called your Reticular Activating System (RAS). This pencil-sized piece of the brain acts as a filter between your senses of touch, taste, sight, and hearing and decides which information goes into your consciousness. Have you ever wondered why you can hear your name above all others in a crowded, noisy room? Or if you're thinking about buying a black car and all of a sudden all you can see are black cars. This filter also tells your brain what is important to you. When you focus on being more positive, your RAS will collect data that confirms this. Conversely, if negativity is deeply ingrained in your personality, you will only hear the bad stuff. Your Reticular Activating System will set your path during the workday & week.

How you feel about the personal & business goals you have set will shape your behavior and decisions. When you and your team have a one-year objective and detailed 90-Day plans, it is easier to focus on the "critical few." Focusing (setting your RAS) on a few critical items you and the team will accomplish sets powerful things in motion. Having a clear focus is a vital part of outstanding Leadership.

# LET'S TAKE ACTION

- How many goals do you have? Hint, you should have no more than three plus a personal goal.

- Post these goals throughout your business/department. Track the progress on these goals publicly for all to see!

# CHAPTER 30
# SMART GOALS

WHEN YOU ARE leading a team, department, or company, you need to have goals that are SPECIFIC, MEASURABLE, ACHIEVABLE, RESULTS oriented, and have a TIME frame attached.

Let's use an example. Your company wants to increase the leads coming from their website. While increasing leads generated from your website *is* a goal, there is no way to measure whether or not you have reached that goal. If you use the SMART goal system, your goal might look something like this:

*Using a contract firm, we will increase the number of website leads from 80/month to 120/month by 1/1/23.*

This goal has a time frame (1/1/23), a starting and ending point (80/month to 120/month), and the goal is not so outlandish that the team might see it as something that cannot be achieved. Once your plan is written, set up systems to track your progress.

# LET'S TAKE ACTION

- Go through your current goals and use the SMART acronym to determine if your goals fit the template. If not, do some work to make each one SMART.

- A SMART goal template is available on our website http://honesttruthbook.com/resources

- Teach this to your leadership team.

# CHAPTER 31
# GROWTH OF YOUR BUSINESS

WE ARE FREQUENTLY asked about a reasonable growth rate in a business. Although it may be somewhat industry-specific, we believe you should set your sights between 12-20%. Look at the growth of your specific industry using trade publications, economic reports, and other readily available data. As a leader in your business, we believe you should expect a better return on your effort. You have placed it all on the line for your business, including your money, time, health, and relationships. With this in mind, expect a higher return, & you'll be amazed at what having those expectations can do. If your goal does not make you uncomfortable, it is probably too small!

# LET'S TAKE ACTION

- Take a look at your growth goal – what if you doubled/tripled it?

- What would it take to get that done? Would it require extra staff? A new physical space? Tools? Technology?

# CHAPTER 32
# MEETINGS

PART OF YOUR leadership role is to ensure you have enough meetings to efficiently transfer information that your team members need to know. We also want to minimize the amount of valuable time spent in meetings. We suggest an annual evaluation of your daily, weekly, monthly, quarterly, and yearly meetings.

For each meeting,

- Is there a clear business purpose and expected result?

- Do the attendees reflect the needs of your growing business?

- Should the outcomes/actions/data be shared with others in the organization?

Just because a meeting has "always" been an hour, it may not need to be. Each session should have an "owner/facilitator" who keeps the conversation on track. Your employees will thank you for ensuring that all of your company meetings are effective and efficient.

# LET'S TAKE ACTION

- Create a spreadsheet of all your meetings with a column for purpose, the attendees, amount of time and the dollar value.

- Calculate the value of all your meetings and put a dollar figure next to each. One way you can do this it to calculate the hourly rate of each person in the room. Next is to ask yourself, is this meeting delivering the value of $X? If it isn't it is time for a change!

# CHAPTER 33
# HANDLING A CRISIS

CRISIS HAPPENS IN every business. It could be a loss of a significant client, illness or death of a team member, an accident, a global pandemic, or a severe economic downturn. When a crisis happens, priority number one is to stay calm. Remember, you are always leading! Your team takes many of their cues from you.

Next is to gather the facts. Focusing on facts, and getting all of the accurate information, helps separate rumors from opinions. Get the right team members involved early to discuss what is known and the options to move forward. Involving the team will help you get things done quicker, prevent confusion, and secure buy-in on the solution. While making decisions, remember priority one is staying *calm*. You panic; they panic.

Evaluate potential solutions and document the action plan as it develops. Always create a communication plan for other employees, customers, sub-contractors, or anyone interested in the outcome. Keeping them informed from the start will save you time and prevent speculation. When communicating to employees, customers, and critical vendors, remember that they all take their cues from your calm demeanor and confidence.

# LET'S
# TAKE ACTION

- Make your own contingency plan to help you be more prepared.

- Make a list of potential crises (I.e., 30% loss in business or a key employee leaves)

- Create action items that would minimize the effects on your business. Get your team involved.

# CHAPTER 34
# SUCCESSION

AS A BUSINESS owner, we encourage you to begin planning for your exit from the business 8-10 years before you leave. Set a timeframe for retirement, and work backward when developing your plans. Doing this well will minimize your tax burden, eliminate potential conflict, and maximize your payoff potential. Each of the many businesses that we've helped with Exit Planning has unique challenges, needs, and opportunities.

There are four major options to exit your business gracefully and profitably:

1. Sell to outsiders
2. Sell to insiders
3. Transfer to family members
4. Create an ESOP – Employee Stock Ownership Plan

Each of these has positives and potential risks. This is an essential process for you and your loved ones. We encourage you to take ownership of this entire process and start early to maximize your happiness throughout the process. Consult with financial experts, and don't forget the team culture, Leadership, and systems that could easily break down in these transitions. That way, you can exit the business gracefully and leave your legacy as a great leader intact.

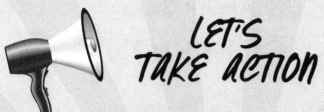

# LET'S TAKE ACTION

- Take the time to read and educate yourself about each option.

- Pick one choice and create a plan with the end goal in mind.

# THE HONEST TRUTH

THE HONEST TRUTH is that all Leaders can be rock stars, including you! We work with the best of the best and help them get better every day.

Congratulations to you for taking the next step to Expert Leadership – reading this book! Cheers!

In addition to the homework you have throughout this book, you have one more assignment. Reward yourself! When you meet the goals you've set out to accomplish, take time to reward yourself for making it that far. Write down the reward when you set the goal so you can be laser-focused on achieving it. That reward could be anything, big or small. A pint of Jeni's ice cream (a Columbus, Ohio specialty), the latest iPhone, a night out with your spouse, a dream vacation, you name it.

We're celebrating with you and cheering you on!

# ARE YOU READY?

Join us on the journey to Expert Leadership! To help along the way, we've got some FREE GIFTS for you. These bonus resources are yours; no obligation necessary.

**Visit WWW.FREEGIFTFROMMYCOACH. COM/HONESTTRUTH or scan the QR Code below.**

# CONNECT WITH US

Follow ActionCOACH Columbus on
Facebook
http://facebook.com/takeactionohio

Follow ActionCOACH Columbus on
Instagram
http://instagram.com/actioncoach614

Join our community on Facebook
https://www.facebook.com/groups/
honesttruthbusiness

Connect with Peg on LinkedIn
https://www.linkedin.com/in/pegbuehrle/

Connect with Pete on LinkedIn
https://www.linkedin.com/in/coachpeter/

# MEET PETE MCDOWELL

**http://petemcdowell.com**

PETE IS CO-MANAGING partner of ActionCOACH Columbus, a global award-winning coaching firm in Columbus, Ohio. He is a recovering chemical engineer who spent over 20 years managing operations in chemical plants for Stauffer Chemical Co. and Occidental Petroleum. He graduated with a degree in Chemical Engineering from Clarkson University and has an MBA from Capital University. Pete has a home on Apple Valley Lake near Howard, Ohio, and enjoys boating, skiing, and anything involving the outdoors. He has three grown children with whom he enjoys traveling. Pete is passionate about helping people leverage their strengths to improve business performance. He believes in increasing business results by focusing on how we interact and communicate with other people. His direct professional experience is in manufacturing, but he understands that as we help others succeed, our business will succeed in any industry. Pete was recently awarded the Global Highest Client Retention award and is proud to lead the team ranked first in the United States and third in the world among the thousands of ActionCOACH franchisees.

# MEET PEG BUEHRLE

**http://pegbuehrle.com**

PEG IS CO-MANAGING partner of ActionCOACH Columbus, a global top 10 coaching firm based in Columbus, Ohio. She spent over 20 years in the radio industry managing large teams of sales professionals. She created many non-traditional revenue streams for her stations and managed the business activities of two popular Columbus stations. Peg is a graduate of The Ohio State University with a degree in Journalism. She lives in Upper Arlington with her husband John, two teenage daughters, two dogs, and two cats. Peg is very competitive, works out daily, is an avid cyclist, and continues to coach and play basketball. Peg is a coach who focuses on improving and leveraging people skills to achieve dramatic business results. She has spent more than 14 years as a coach helping busy executives increase their effectiveness, and business owners improve results with less effort. Peg develops very close relationships with her clients and helps them do the same with their employees. Peg mentors other coaches from all over the world who want to learn from her. Peg was recently awarded the Smart 50 award for leading one of the Smartest companies in the region; the Global Biggest Community Impact award is proud to lead the team ranked first in the United States and third in the world among the thousands of ActionCOACH franchisees.